PRAISE FOR *SAD ANIMAL*

"'Emphatic / breathing in all sound makes / a vatic wail.' Channeling Gerard Manley Hopkins, McKinney turns the agonistic questions of faith from the inside to the outside: devotions in the day, the small graces of sunlight, 'shook foil,' on not only the texture of the landscape, but the hide of memory. 'The shadow casts the man.' Yet attention matters, makes things prayer. Ekphrastic, intertextual, formally precise, McKinney's *Sad Animal* finds its deep measure in the imbricated organ of our times, 'where plume-sheen / dazzles in last light / and my ravening, / parched heart leaps // into the air.'"

—Matthew Cooperman
    author of *the atmosphere is not a perfume it is odorless*

Published by Gunpowder Press
David Starkey, Editor
PO Box 60035
Santa Barbara, CA 93160-0035

Front cover image: *Enkeli* by Samuli Heimonen
© 2024 Artists Rights Society (ARS), New York / KUVASTO, Helsinki

Author photo by Selena McKinney

ISBN-13: 978-1-957062-16-7

www.gunpowderpress.com

Sad Animal

Poems

Joshua McKinney

Gunpowder Press • Santa Barbara
2024

For my mother

CONTENTS

And all is seared with trade; bleared, smeared with toil;
 And wears man's smudge and shares man's smell: the soil
Is bare now, nor can foot feel, being shod.

And for all this, nature is never spent;
 There lives the dearest freshness deep down things;

—Gerard Manley Hopkins

Anniversary

I sit facing my father, naked
in his new suit. His hands rest on his knees, fingers
slick with birthblood. If he moves,

his wicker chair creaks
like an exhausted barn, his white hair flares
like the first word of a struck match.

My father sits facing me, young
in my new suit, my dark hair orphaned to rage.
My hands are black with grave dirt.

Each of us has something to say.
As schooled, I look him in the eyes
where two mules pull a plow through snow.

He stands up, young and handsome
in his blue suit, his hair
dark as barn smoke. *Papa*, he says.

My wicker chair creaks.
My white hair flares like the first word
of a struck match, which is also its last.

Stone Sijo

Stones teach us to make things fit,
      as a cairn will make us choose,
as best we can, to form the shape
      seen in the mind. But shapes can change.
One might say *stone* in this place or *rock* in that
      to mark the path of a thought.

One might say *rock* in this place
      or *stone* in that, if the sound sounds
smooth or rough on the lithe tongue,
      hot or cold in the live ear.
And all this is due to what each stone gives
      or does not give. Stones do not take.

If you learn, you will know this.
      If you learn, with a quick tongue,
to speak the speech of hard, still stone,
      then you will know the one earth-truth.
Ask a stone to tell you what it means to be stone,
      and you will know. Stone turns to stone.

I have heard some say that stones
      lack mind, lack life—hence we say *stone-*
cold, stone-deaf, stone-blind—but those whose words
      say such things do not know stones.
Go, go there, where stones lie, and look
      at the hill stones, creek stones, sea stones.

Hear each stone—hill stone, creek stone,
      sand stone, sea stone, strong stone, hard stone,
sand or soap stone, bone-of-earth stone—
      tell their stone tales, how they came there.
Then, at last, stone-taught, steeped in stone-fact, sing
      the first low note of your own stone-song.

Catechism

Unheard until now,
        this morning's chickadee,

and then the garbage truck's
        pneumatic arm exhales

a crash of glass. Emphatic
        breathing in all sound makes

a vatic wail, a free decree
        in the mild tenacity of waking,

the warm alarm of the child-
        world continually teething.

What has so cursed us as to make
        such first occurrence old?

Once, when I was born, I nursed
        awhile, and then, ungrieving

for some future loss, forgot.
        Music burns in me

as in the bones of the little bird outside.

Thaw

Two whole days I stand staring
           down into the round black hole
I have bored through the lake ice.
           Ice mountains blaze all around.
Inside me something cracks in the stillness.
           Two trout lie gutted in new snow.

A Prognosis

an evening scent of rain
under the moon's trampled shine

a rat scurries off to night school
across the high wire where moments ago

your voice in blue gauze let fall
winter and I caught nothing at all

somewhere my phantom limb gestures
obscenely somewhere

there are other words besides
on the broken stones

Down River

Then he said   there

                where the water   widened

grew shallow

           under the shadow of the bluff   there

the surface burned   the eyes   as scales

    blazed   and you could   wade   out   among them

as among a herd   and feel

                the current   the whole of them

   move

and numb

        from the knees

                down

reach in   and stroke   their bright sides   and feel them

      shudder   under your hands there

in the Klamath

        when the salmon ran   there

    when he was young

Bode

Betimes on the morning of the day
        the god was to receive its office
                at the hands of the people,
there came at once something like fire.

The sun, without ire, ascended. Ships stopped
        to unload dark cargo into the sea.
                No one noticed
the absence of birds. For a time,

I saw the child's eye shine under the steeple,
        then falter as his blocks toppled. He ran out
                into the street, halted
where the flame had been.

How I Lost My Voice

1
A naughty child has left
night's door ajar.
In a sepia waking
my mother slams that door,
its porcelain knob tethered
to my loose tooth.
By this method, my tongue
is taught to be still.

2
At the kitchen sink,
my grandmother's arthritic
claws scurry over the board
where a headless capon
crows a final, defiant boast,
that converges with blood-
tongues to circle, backwards,
down the drain's dark throat.
Thus I am taught to devour silence.

3
After Sunday school, I build
a Tinker Toy Tower of Babel.
In my myth, I scale the gleaming walls
of curiosity's cabinet, where
tiny skulls lurk among labels
and the aspirin tastes like oranges.
Discovered by Mother, I confess
I swallowed one, and one

only, to soothe a toothache.
Her unbelieving fingers force me
to vomit up the truth. I must wait,
I am told, for my father's return.
Thus I am taught the efficacy of lies.

4
The rooted force the rootless
to release their hold. Each
new tooth rises like a headstone
in a graveyard of dead speech.
As the years progress,
they grow crowded, topple.
Words wear away. The tongue
lies in the mouth like a corpse
in a coffin. Thus I learn
the limits of metaphor.

5
In the final stanza, I sit
alone an in empty room
lit by a pill-sized moon.
I hold one end of a pale thread.
It winds across the floor
into darkness, where its end
is tied to the bone knob
of Death's open door.
I open my mute mouth wide,
tie my end in a tiny noose
around my last loose tooth.

Nursery

There are those who debate
the merits of talking
to houseplants. Some say
the carbon dioxide is beneficial.
Some say the vibration of
70 decibels activates genes
involved in light response.
I say merely talking is not sufficient.
What one says, however, is
primary. I berate mine. It takes
a special variety to flourish.
The insipid geranium, the lazy
Christmas cactus, the plain ficus,
the chubby aloe. None of them
survive. Only the miniature
rose proves strong enough
to take what I dish out.
It grows until its blooms
are big as truck tires, its thorns
long as a pit bull's fangs.
It no longer requires sunlight.
I keep it down in the basement,
which used to be
my daughter's room.

Lesson

One can learn from a downpour:

        You can run from eave to eave

in a manner undignified,

        or you can stride straight down the road.

Either way, you get the same soaking.

        This applies to all things.

March

Under mud and brittle leaves,
in a month named for war,

> the throes of spring begin,
> ecstatic and adorned for war.

Behold the hordes stumbling
in cracked earth, clutching

> their children, torn, numb.
> They will be blamed for war.

Of the estimated 500 million
firearms worldwide, 100 million

> belong to the Kalashnikov family,
> a family famed for war.

Behold the desperate vessel
tossed at sea, the tiny body

> on the beach. For what
> are we thus shamed? For war?

The nominee presumed
to know the people's needs.

> In fact, he understood their fear.
> So he campaigned for war.

Consider the irony
in the nomenclature of genocide:

        Apache, Kiowa, Chinook, Tomahawk.
        We use these names for war.

In Belgium, 1915, poppies
dotted the shattered fields.

        In Kandahar, 2016—a sea
        of poppies farmed for war.

The slogan reads *Our Children,*
Our Future. But the displaced

        children cannot read—
        an entire generation claimed for war.

The ex-soldier cannot sleep.
He is afraid of crowds, loud noises,

        even trash. Is this what it means
        to be trained for war?

Does anyone care that a short-
tailed bandicoot rat went extinct

        when the Mesopotamian Marshes
        were drained for war?

The ancient Romans extolled
the virtues of spring, a time

when earth, and so men's hearts,
grew warm for war.

Even I, Kafir, nonbeliever
that I am, can see the coming

of a time when all months
shall be renamed for war.

Eco-nomics

Semper Idem

Drenched by breach-clouds,
        the crustose lichens turn—

                        drunk with rain and
                  dappling the rocks—to fire

        in their bright course
                through the halls
      of granite.

In wind-hewn lashes,
        the lichens' cup-shaped
apothecia release
        a boundless spore-fleet that
                    sails off
                      toward distant latitudes.

        If they survive to land
on alien substrates,
           they send out hyphae,
      capture algae,
erect a fungal thallus—
                within those mountain walls,
            renamed now as *photobionts*,

their indigenous forms
      distorted, the algae labor,
           rendering food from light.

Credential

I was born in Iowa, which is to say that I, too, attended
the Iowa Writers' Workshop. I spent my formative years
sitting cross-legged and hunched amid straight rows of corn
that stretched to the level edge of the horizon.

I was schooled in the stoic doctrine of a scarecrow
wearing my dead grandfather's overalls, my dead aunt's straw hat.
I grew silent reciting my primer to a one-eyed crow:
A is for Alfalfa; B is for Blizzard; C is for Corn.

Unshod and shirtless, I was lashed by the summer sun's ferule
until sheets of skin hung from my back like wallpaper
in a dead farmhouse. These my mother peeled away
and pressed in a Bible, and on these I composed my first poem,

an ode to how no one wept when my father left
his tractor ticking in the field and walked off over the broken earth
into the arms of a waitress waiting with her herbs and erasures.
No one took offense at the insinuation of wild rose

mounting the trellis by the well, or when the evening breeze
brought rumor of swine from the neighboring farm.
Although she strove to conceal it, I knew my mother
was a muskrat, for I had spied her rise sleek-furred and dripping

from the creek, crunching a crayfish in her teeth.
Oh, halcyon days of metamorphosis and theft! At times,
there were raccoons in the corn crib, hornets in the outhouse,
foxes in the henhouse. There were, at times, opossums

in the corn crib, skunks in the hothouse, raccoons in the outhouse,
foxes in the henhouse. Other times, there were mice

in the corn crib, hornets in the hothouse, foxes, raccoons,
and skunks in the henhouse. Once, I even caught my granny

sucking eggs in the henhouse, but that became our bond
and no one was harmed. Come winter, the cold smacked me
around until my nose dripped to my lips and froze.
The sleeves of my jacket were snail-tracked with snot.

My cheeks chapped as I tracked myself down the ice-
packed storm-cellar path for a jar of sunlight and syrup.
I gobbled apricot cobbler and green beans and dreamed of
a time when the glass world would shatter and I could

launch a fleet of paper boats in the horse trough.
When spring set the trees and eaves to weeping, I made
mud pies and fed my slipper to a sow. And when at last
the grass erased it all with green, I escaped my personality,

and my degree was conferred. All this was a long time ago,
I remember, as I stand on the beach and gaze across
a wind-harrowed sea to the convex western edge of the horizon.
But set down this, set down this: my tutelage cost nothing

save the smell of silage, the sight of my granny
come lumbering from the barn, a pail of moonlight
in each hand. My only assignment was to rise as nobody
from my cot on the screen-porch where I tossed

in the fever of night's damp dog-mouth, to rise and run
barefoot under a sky so sprent with stars they sank to earth,
where I plucked them from their erratic orbits and held them
in loose devotion, pulsing and luminescent, their greeny light
leaking through the fingers of my sticky, anonymous fists.

American Idiom

When I was a boy and playground squabbles grew
too heated, our last resort was to evoke
the power of our fathers and to boast,
"My dad can whip your dad." If it wasn't true,
it hardly mattered because somehow, we knew,
or couldn't know, that men would never come to blows
over what we said behind the jungle gym. We spoke
freely, not knowing that our tongues could do

far more than fists. There was a brutal fluency
that we absorbed at home, immersed in words
condensed to violent metaphors; they colored
speech with the hue of our community.
In time we'd learn to wield a lexicon of slurs,
and thus, to love our kind, united in identity.

Jubilate

When Smart fell to his mad knees,
            in public, and prayed aloud—
a deranged, unfashionable,
            sad animal—they locked him up.
Here am I, Lord, shouting in this madhouse, though
            I've yet to rout the company.

Elsewhere

a man is pounding his pain
into his girlfriend
from behind, forcing her

face into the carpet, while
elsewhere a man hurls
a hammer at the stained

glass window he has hung
himself in his own
house, while elsewhere

in a barnyard a man is beating
the hood of his truck
with a hay hook, while

elsewhere a man discovers
his right fist concealed
behind the plaster and lath

of a tenement wall and
while his wife and children
cower in the corner

he eases it out through
the hole in the silence and
stares in horror at the bloody

fivefold secret of himself
like some strange and intimate
message left by the builder.

His name,

for it will be a *he*, shall not be spoken.
His face shall not be known.
In his latest incarnation, he walks among us

even now, incapable of being seen
by those whom he envies or despises, covets or fears—
and by those of us who have forsaken him

as something beyond comprehension. And yet,
we know him in the abstract, statistical aftermath;
he will be white, approximately nineteen.

He will, most likely, use a handgun or
an AR-15. The clerk who will sell it to him,
when facts are traced and blame is laid,

will claim adherence to the law. Cast out
into a virtual world, in his pain he will plot
with his peers in the guise of a game,

and his screen name will reveal to them
his slow-unfolding plan. Apostles to his twisted creed,
only they will see the signs. Only they

will believe, and their silence, like our own,
will ensure his purpose is achieved.
At the appointed time, few who look upon his face

will live. And even after he commits the act,
to him the sacrifice of self, even then
we will refuse to see. In our righteous anger

we will refuse to grant him infamy.
We will shun his image, expunge his name
from record and report, and we will try,

as we are destined to, to triumph over
what he represents—the violent privation
of our private selves, the stark revelation

of who we are and who we have become.
And we will fail again, as we are destined to fail,
and his name will remain, his name

will live on, whispered in chat rooms
among the anonymous faithful, howled
in the vengeful prayers of the stricken.

Psalm

If we ascend, you are still there.

    If we descend, still you remain.

If we take wings, or oily fins,

    where shall we flee from your presence?

O Plastic, enduring surrogate god,

    you are with us to the world's end.

Waiting to View the Corpse Flower

No sooner had the warm liquid, and the crumbs with it, touched my palate than a shudder ran through my whole body, and I stopped, intent upon the extraordinary changes that were taking place.

—Marcel Proust

Outside Sequoia Hall, the line is long, and long the wait to get inside, long
    as the interval between blooms, or so it seems to seem to the troops
      of children, jostling with the twitchy joy of having
        ridden the bus away from school.

          Scores of others

have joined the throng, attracted by the putrid spectacle, this thing we may not live to see
    again. In groups of ten we're ushered in to cluster at the perforated glass,
      while the attendant graduate student explains,

        for the fiftieth time today, the way the frilly spathe
          yawns wide, revealing

its crimson interior, and how the spike-like fetid spadix, erect as an obelisk, stands for a day,
    then withers and dies back, the dormant corm waiting to begin
      a new cycle. A team from KCRA is here, vying for the scoop—
        "this rare event that people are 'dying' to witness."

An elderly couple

has driven up from Fresno to cross it off their bucket list. They have waited for years,

they say, to see one, and would have flown to Chicago if they hadn't missed

that brief bloom. "I wanted to see," says a fourth-grade boy,

mic thrust in his face, "if it actually smells

like a dead body."

He assures his grinning buddies that it does, while near him, a girl in a hijab stands still,

her gaze chained to something far beyond these walls, something far

beyond description. As she turns to hurry out, I see her back-

pack is embroidered with the name Hayat.

When my turn comes,

I focus, try to retain the alien, rare, and beautiful bloom of a plant driven to near extinction

by coal mining in Harapan, by illegal logging in Gunung Terang.

And the smell? *Amorphophallus titanum* is, as far as my nose

knows, close enough to carrion, like roadkill on

a sweltering day,

a day like today, like yesterday, like tomorrow . . . the forecast is filled with them.

If this corpse flower lives to bloom again, it's likely I'll be gone.

Walking back to class, I pass the waiting line stretched out

across the concrete quad, quaking in the heat, and

I cannot help

35

but think of the line for the next spectacle, a decade hence, how the savor of death

will draw a new throng, and I cannot help but think of those de-composed from

that crowd when they are finally allowed inside the climate-

controlled room to gather at the glass.

What children, riven

from what land? What Chitumebi, what Boon-Nam, what Daryna, what Daw? What Jacinta?

What Jesús? To where will they return, reluctant, hurled by the taste of their past,

a homing scent that quickens the pulse and sends dread

crawling through the heart like a beetle

across a blind eye?

When Paradise Burned

—The Camp Fire, Butte Co., California, 2018

we felt it though we were far away. We awoke
to the smoke from that great blaze, those of us
who thought they might have passed that way

once upon a time, those who said they knew
the region well, and those who said they doubted
there had ever been a place so named. My friends,

smoke made the invisible air visible until
the void between things grew thick with absence.
We could no longer ignore it: there is no *away*.

At night we gathered around our screens, stared
into the images of fire and listened to the stories
of destruction, of bright-helmed fighters and the dead.

And we were warned to stay indoors, told
breathing was a hazard. People wore masks
when going to work or to Walmart, as if

in a time of contagion. Neighbors, it touched us all,
of that we had no doubt. For a time, even the young
among us took on a new awareness of air,

of breath, of how we were drawing into ourselves
things transformed in the flames, entire towns
incinerated, their components rendered particulate—

plastic and asbestos and heavy metals—(*Toxic*
was voted Word of the Year). Red-eyed, choking,
we recalled the First Law: stripped of its bonds,

matter changes form yet is conserved. And yes,
my friends, as the death toll rose we thought, yes,
we thought about the dead. We took them in, too.

Bound to those others, though they were gone,
we carried them within us, the body's burden
born of destruction. We had seen the survivors

grieving on our screens, their faces twisted
in the strange chemistry of mourning: grief and rage and
grief and rage and grief again. And neighbors,

it wasn't long before the many questions became
one: Where had such violence come from? How
to lay that burden down? In short, who was to blame?

My friends, even in the thick of it, I saw a man
running in shorts and Nikes down the street, still
training for something against all sense,

his desire to thrive so strong it could kill him.
And every afternoon as I sat at my desk
by the window, I would see Swanson, my neighbor

across the street, his wife near nine months
dead of lung cancer, totter out of his house to observe
his ritual of raking the yard. It being late fall,

his lone maple had long since lost its leaves.
Yet there he was, fragile, out in the smoke raking,
a cigarette in his mouth, adding smoke to smoke.

Neighbors, I knew his wife. She never smoked.
It was a revelation to me: the contour of that terrible
circle, destroyed and destroying, at once a spurring

and a reining back. What had the land to grieve,
to grieve that it was filled with such rage?
When Paradise burned we became lost in the ghost

of that place, lost without it, and grief and rage
were like breathing, an instinctive thing. And when at last
the fire passed and the smoke cleared and we could breathe

again freely, the ghost of that smoke remained
in our clothes, in our hair, as if its origin was
within us, and we would have to bear it

unto our last inspiring, the understanding that
there is no transcendence, that we had been pulled
down with a smoke that in us refuses to rise. Friends,

we are banished from ourselves by fire that knows
no season, driven by a gale that gathers all we have
lost and, howling, returns it, saying, "Take this: know

now, there are multitudes inside you—grass and trees,
deer and bear, and untold others—and somewhere deep,
dark as the heart's den, a knot of vipers, the nerve

fibers of their pit-organs firing at the heat of the future's
furious approach, a future you must yield to, a future
before which you find yourselves foiled, fallen

under the weight of the once ungrievable world.
Take this knowledge you refuse to know. Take this,
this unbearable thing. Now it belongs to you."

Novum

When the turning season came,
                we wondered what it meant.
        Nature's thin veneer was stripped away—
stunned leaves sundered from their trees,
                    divided without consent.
And then a white silence fell,
      heavy, drifting to the eaves of houses
                    where families prayed their prayers for snow,
nature's thin veneer.   Stripped away,
           the stunned leaves faded to memory
and were gone. Somehow, we'd forgotten
           how to feel.   Our numb blood fumbled
                through the narrow halls of houses
      where families prayed. Their prayers for snow
           were answered by a warm wind that
raised seas, sparked wars, starved millions,
           stripped away any awareness of suffering.
                        To feel our numb blood fumbling
      through the narrow halls of our veins became
              an addiction, the brain's slow buffering
in the long longing days of distortion.

           The ragged mourned.   Millions starved.
               Stripped away, any awareness of suffering
was a dead leaf banished by a warm wind.
           Deaf to the alarm, when the turning season came
we wondered what it meant.
        In the long longing days of distortion,
            the ragged mourned,
sundered from their trees, divided
        without consent.

Epiphany

I was ten when my dog died,
            run over by a bread truck.
She lay there in the street, still
            the same dog, yet different.
I knew then that the difference
            was everything, was the soul.

Suzerain

Foremost, the known world un-nouned—
        then the compulsion to claim
    by sound the rights of
          souls moving through
      dew-sprent grass. The bright afterbirth dimmed,

and each creature, tamed,
        crept into the cage
    of its name. He found
         he could no longer cry
      without grief, no longer howl without atrocity.
The sun-shocked grass hissed
      before the wind, his prior voice
    sloughed in a bramble of
         equivocation and deceit.

Then his new tongue grew
      mute with its wealth of
  words, the world weary with looking.
         He turned and, in loneliness
     imperishable, made a new third thing.
Salmon arced like arrows
      against the falls; a tiger unsheathed the bright
  blades of its claws.

Homage to Thomas Traherne in the Pyrocene

Manuscripts don't burn.
                                    —Mikhail Bulgakov

On the road from Lancashire, a man saved God
            from a trash fire, where blackening pages
curled, the heat-cracked hydrocarbons unmade,
            then made again in destruction's bright image.

It was such heat and light drew my first eyes
            away from paradise. And when at last
I saw again, earth's beauty was ablaze
            beyond change. Candled in catastrophe, it cast

no promise of a further birth. I thought
            of all that had been lost, the hidden book
engulfed within each tree—how I was not
            recorded there—such immaculate lack as to wake

the glowing ember of God in a trash fire,
            or the incandescent soul of the late earth's pyre.

Patriotism

Some say the world will end in fire,
Some say in ice.

—Robert Frost

My father used to say he loved his country,
by which he meant the land
between the Klamath Mountains and
the Modoc Plateau, from the Oregon border
to the southern tip of the cascades
and the mountain the Karuk called Úytaahkoo.

He roamed that region for years, took
Sabbath there regardless of the day,
and tried to know its living things—except
the goddamned people. He'd walk ten wordless miles,
then stop to drink or mend a cairn and drop some
scrap of thought. Then he'd set off again, quickened,

as if his speech had broken something
more than silence. There was often a boy
behind him, struggling to keep pace, footsore
and afraid that in those high places
lightning lurked in the boiling clouds.
What boy's father isn't a god for a time?

When my father died, we brought home his effects.
The clothes he'd worn, folded in a paper bag,
still held the scent of sweat and ponderosa pine.
Such smells, he said, a man could draw into himself
and hold and know he was alive. Today

I followed those words up Shasta until
they vanished in an air so thin my burning
lungs felt void. Inspired, I stood looking down
at the country I'd come from, choked
in the wildfire haze. From off the waning glacier,
a cold wind came whistling its ragged
anthem, which in time, tatters all flags.

Un-selfie

The meadow full of flowers
            and dawn-light does not need me.
The mountain, its summit crowned
            in trackless snow, does not need me.
No witness to my presence is required.
            In my absence I was there.

Null Choir

I saw the silence there
the looking bird
bristling on old snow and I
knew the sound of your voice

desired a little word
that I might through it escape
unto you in your
terrible sentence without verb

then through the first circle
of the raven's eye
I heard the "is" erased as first
light pierced suddenly

the field edgeless
in a silence the sheer
unspeakable color
had devoured

Why I Sleep in My Best Suit

Because if I wake up, I am
already dressed. Call it
efficiency, this refusal to fritter
a day with unnecessary
dressing, which act, completed
at morn, must then at eve
be undone. Because
as my granny used to say,
what starts as a jaunt
to the market for eggs might
end with you splayed and
broken in the street. Ergo:
make sure you have clean
undies on. Because each night,
when I take the train to search
for you, the somber porter with
the pointy teeth allows me
to ride for free. Because
your time zone is invisible.
Because when the coyotes
wake me with their collect calls
and I run into the desert and
hold the cactus flower to my
ear, I think I can hear you
smiling behind the frigid
frequency of crickets.
Because it forces me to fight
wrinkles, lying on my back,
hands crossed at the spot

where the heart's wicket was
kicked in. Because that dark
blue pinstripe stands out
amid the ice floes on a king-
size sea. Because eventually,
I will be handed an instrument
of uncertain use. Because
it's warm.

Fabric

Black and white, my earliest memories
are stitched together by the whir and click
of my grandmother's Singer 66. She kept me
clothed—through the corn-silk heat of Iowa
summers to the snow-blind winters with ruptured
water pipes. She followed patterns she bought
at the Ben Franklin, but also those handed down.

Afternoons, I'd wake from my nap
to that chugging sound, follow it down
the hall to her sewing room where I'd find
her hunched over the machine, feet pumping
the treadle, right hand on the wheel as if
chained to the thing. Wedded at thirteen,
widowed young, she lived alone for thirty years,

and while my parents worked, she cared for me,
her kindness a balm for my father's
anger at the world. At her funeral
someone said that in the 30's she'd fed men
who'd hopped off freight cars, hungry, heading
to Omaha and beyond to look for work.
All agreed that she was a "good woman."

I'd known nothing of her life before
those years when I sat on the floor beside her
while she sewed—piloting the silver rocket
of a spare bobbin, stacking wooden thread spools
amid fabric scraps and bolts of new cloth with
its faint formaldehyde smell—lulled by the
soothing music of that big machine.

If I was good, she'd take me to her bedroom,
and allow me to gaze at the whatnot
shelf my late grandfather built. It housed
an odd collection of marvels: a pewter bowl of
marbles made from kiln-fired clay,
a walrus tusk scrimshawed with a scene
of a whaling bark at sea, a stuffed baby

crocodile. There was a child-sized iron cast
in solid iron and a family of dolls dressed
in bright embroidered gowns, their pink porcelain
faces hand-painted, their faded blue eyes
staring out from beneath veils of finest
cracks. But the item I remember most,
among those wonders, was a cup-sized china

toilet, with a lid you could actually lift
to reveal, hiding naked inside, a small black boy.
He squatted there, looking up, grinning with huge
cartoonish teeth and eyes—an expression
unnatural, stuck between fright and impish glee.
When I asked my grandmother why the boy
was in there, she said, "Isn't that the cutest thing?"

Reap

The next fire, in the black weeds,

        whispers prayers for the last fire.

I can hear it hiss with slim tongues

        of green flame in the spring grass.

Soon, I ween that seeds of fire will spark a harvest,

        the brightest dark revelation.

The Funeral of Shelley

Louis Edouard Fournier 1889

As Fournier composed the scene, the body
lies serene upon a pyre. A trace of flame
licks over Shelley's shoulder, and smoke frames
his pale seraphic face. To the left, Trelawny,
Hunt, and Byron stand. The latter's eyes trail
skyward, as if to mark the rising flight
of some blithe spirit. Further left, in gothic light
at canvas-edge, a grieving Mary kneels

in prayer. In truth, she was not even there.
Such is the power of calculated art,
which can relimb a putrid wreck of flesh,
restore a face, preserve a charnel heart,
and thus corrupt what actually occurred:
they looked upon that carcass and despaired.

In Perpetuum

> *As he burned he never moved a muscle, never uttered a sound, his outward*
> *composure in sharp contrast to the wailing people around him.*
> —David Halberstam

Some images enter the eye and remain,
as if carved in an arc of the skull's dome, or folded
in some furrow of the brain. Like the pyre

of Thích Quảng Đức, whose indelible form
I've retained for more than fifty years,
those placid features holding my child-eyes

still, as frozen amid tongues of corybantic flame
he sits silent and unmoving, save for
the raging action of his stillness. The living

heat arrested as, leaping, it seizes him, appears
also to emanate from the monk as if some long restraint
has given way, the flames bursting forth and

absconding skyward with the coiling smoke.
Thus the stunned aperture captures a world
in black and white, no color and all color,

the timeless past before us both reflected
and absorbed. And now, in vivid hues, one tower explodes,
as its twin spews forth a poisonous woad that

inscribes the air with death not fated or deserved
and leads the heart down paths of grim foreboding.
Nearby, the second plane looms in perpetuum.

I close my eyes and the walls of that cave where
the mind hides are scripted over with pictures
flickering in the glow of the sole, devouring

constant: a splendid violence without restraint.
One conflagration's self-sacrifice is another's
suicide, each bedight in its own fierce light,

each gasping a last breath to waft its own sad
anthem of ash. I close my eyes and witness.
I bow to the radiant horror of the martyr, all

those beautiful humans with their flesh on fire.

Omen

Tossed in the surf, the first turned up along the coast in June. Soon, our talk flew in whispers concerning what it might mean. And when the numbers grew, as they did each day thereafter, it wasn't long before the only question amid the discord was who to blame. Those who wanted proof made their way to the sea. Some came from afar to boast of their disbelief. These left in tears. Others claimed a grief in knowing all along, yet left unsure of what they'd seen. And still more washed ashore and no one knew why they came or from where.

The Word

In my mouth I hold the word
               for the word I want to speak.
But that word, the desired word,
               the shadow word, will break if heard.
So I wait, tonguing the dark word's weight
               in the silence called poetry.

Men of Letters

Tell Patrick for statistics sake Mr. Stevens is 6 feet 2 weighs 225 lbs. and that when he hits the ground it is highly spectaculous.

—Ernest Hemingway in a letter
to Sara Murphy, 1936

Stevens and Hemingway fought in the street.
It was Key West, low elevation and alligators.
Childish perhaps, but I like the story: too much
to drink, some hurtful words, followed by
fists—a contact petty and human.

My mind makes a primal struggle of it,
a great symbolic bout: Poetry vs. Prose.
Knowledge of physics favored the novelist,
who knocked the poet down a time or two.
Yet Stevens broke his hand on Papa's jaw.

Afterward, feeling undignified, they made amends,
constructed a fiction to fit the facts:
Officially, Stevens fell down a flight of stairs.
Tell me reader, if you know, what *compassion* is.
In a mind of winter, I am dreaming of lions.

Copula

what if
if what
we think
is is is
sacred be-
fore the
subject
sucked in-
to predication
completes
any thing?
Or
if *is* is a
bond, band,
what if what
is does is
tie the pliant
spirit of
a person
to the act-
of-being
and so
in fact un-
ties the price-
less is of who
one is, the
Is in any
of us?

The Distance

April 2021

Six feet between us,
we viewed the cherry blossoms.
Defiant beauty.

We laughed behind masks
as pink petals drifted down.
A lone crow had flown.

Six feet between us.
The teacup warm in my hands.
I could smell the sea.

The apparition
of masked faces in a crowd.
When will it be safe?

Supine in the grass,
my body is six feet long.
Why were you the one?

Safe with a vaccine,
in spring I visit your grave.
Six feet between us.

Dream #37

My father and I sit in shade
facing each other, our backs
against the trunks of large, smooth-
barked fruit trees. Beyond him,
a green field frosted with
blossoms, and in the long silences
bees drone over the clover.
I have not seen nor spoken
to my father in forty years.
After so much time, his reasons
for leaving seem irrelevant. What good
would come from accusation?
I have broken promises myself,
and I have come to understand
the inevitability of parting. I tell him
my mother has remarried and
is doing well, that my kids are
grown now and on their own.
"But are they ever, really?" he says.
I pick up a fist-sized windfall fruit,
polish it on my thigh, take a bite.
It has no taste. My father winces.
He looks terrible, and I must look
pretty bad myself. The bees have grown
louder; the air seems to vibrate
with their humming. I know
the question my father wants to ask,
but before he can ask it, a woman
screams, then appears
in full flight, pursued by three pitbulls,

and passes, in a stumbling run, over
a distant hill. "Is it always like this?"
I ask. My father cannot answer.
The tree he leans against reaches
two limbs down and tears open
the stapled suture stretching from
his throat to his naval. A bushel of
fruit spills from his chest cavity, scatters
across the grass like broken
billiard balls. Famished, I clutch at one,
but my mouth is full of bees.
They have found the hole
at the back of my head, and entering there
have built a comb in my skull.
I have not seen nor spoken to my father
in forty years. I cannot speak to him
now. I cannot even see him
for the honey oozing from my eyes.

Shade

A man thinks he owns his form,

          that his shadow is his alone,

that his body, its flesh and bone,

          obstructs the light in his image,

when in fact, he possesses nothing.

          The shadow casts the man.

World Enough

At the department meeting,
I am sitting, back to the wall,
in the back corner of the room,
next to the antique pencil-sharpener
bolted to the wall, its little crank
hanging down at six o'clock,
the hour it has tolled for years.
I am trying to remember Marvell's mistress,
but the lines are coy, coming
to me in pieces, which is, I suppose,
no crime. And there is, after all,
the assistance of rhyme. Now
I find that I am left complaining
by the "tide of Humber," and I wonder
how does it go from there?
Someone is making a motion
to make a motion on a previous
motion, concerning the minutes
from the last meeting, those precious
minutes forever lost, and, ah, yes,
here comes time's wingèd chariot,
with that memorable accented suffix,
interrupted by a cold blast of horns and
motors from the street outside. The Dean
is making a case for cancelling
a poetry class with only twenty-five students.
I suppose I am expected to object,
but the willing soul expires, no,
wait, *transpires*, and I would rather
this moment devour than languish

in the slow-chapped power
of this latest scheme: Tell us, in ten words
or less, why poetry is important,
and we will use it in a student recruitment
campaign on Twitter. I have lost
my youthful hue, it's true, yet
I can still seize these lines from
some recess of my brain, and find
sport amid these monthly deserts
of vast eternity, where I must tear
my pleasure through the iron gates
of budgetary strife. And now I hear
a blessèd movement to adjourn,
and rise to go, reminded yet again,
of the importance of poetry.

(as)under

scaled invention
silly heaven

once blessed or
true artistry

about the flowers
at evening

an hour or two
face down

without words
a mode

of wit a ghost
might use

be found in
what is

far from the eye
pulled down

beneath rafters
of grass

Haibun

I

Typically, by the Fourth of July but depending upon how long and wet the winter was, I start to think of wildflowers. You have to time the bloom-time, which is tied to elevation. The lower-slope species blossom in May or June, and as summer moves along, the colors climb the slopes of the Sierra Nevada. Typically, in the Sacramento Valley, by midsummer, the sun's hammer has gilded the hills with dead grass, and the rivers are clogged with screaming pleasure seekers trying to escape the heat. And typically, word starts to spread among the amateur botanists and hikers and photographers regarding the brilliance and abundance of the year's bloom. In Japan there is a word for it: *hanami*, which literally means "flower viewing," though to the Japanese the term almost always refers to viewing cherry blossoms, or sometimes, plum. Each year the weather bureau issues a blossom forecast or *sakura-zensen*, a "cherry blossom front." For a long time I did not know this.

> Old snow lingers long
> on the ridge to Ellis Peak—
> truant spring, good student.

II

There are facts that we will never know, and our not knowing doesn't
diminish them. The facts remain. And I find my eagerness to know is
greater than it's ever been. Which is why it was particularly delicious to
be there, on the dusty, narrow trail to Ellis Peak, with my daughter, home
for a rare visit, who now knows enough to teach me about wildflowers.
As I followed her up the trail clutching my field guide, she named flowers
from memory, their family, genus, and species. My father could do this,
too, a man dead long before my daughter was born. Watching her, I
imagined my father kneeling next to a flower and thumbing through his
hardcover edition of Munz' *California Flora*, which must have been three
inches thick. And I remembered Larry, my father's friend, asking, voice
rising in exasperation, "What does it matter what someone, somewhere,
sometime decided to call it?" I was in high school, and I recall my father
trying to explain that while common names varied country to country and
region to region, the scientific names remained more or less consistent,
and so formed a kind of universal language. "Yeah," Larry said, "but
only eggheads talk like that." For me, the common names were nearly
always enough, and their variation only made them more appealing.
Listening, they make a kind of music: *yarrow, horsemint, rockcress, crimson
columbine, smokey mariposa, mule's ears, pussypaws, lupine*. And then the
diverse colors which, on a clear day, are so bright they seem to assail the
eye, a word that seems appropriate if you trace its etymology back to
Vulgar Latin: *adsalire*, "to leap at."

>   Tiny crimson doves
>   flush up from the granite scree.
>   Now what was my name?

III

We passed some Indian paintbrush, and my daughter reminded me that it was the first flower I taught her to name, if only commonly. "Paintbrush," she said. "Genus *Castilleia*, though I'm not sure what species." The generic, *Castilleia*, chosen to honor Domingo Castillejo, a Spanish botanist, surgeon, and professor who was a correspondent for the Royal Botanical Garden of Madrid, a position in which he received many plants imported from the New World. Paintbrush was always my favorite Sierra flower, because its name seems to correspond to the array, one might even say *palette*, of bloom-time colors. Many indigenous tribes used paintbrush blossoms for medicinal purposes, hence the term Indian Paintbrush. I offered the fact to my daughter, who knew it already, and as we ate our lunch in the shade of a massive Jeffrey Pine, its south side shagged with wolf lichen glowing its bright, almost fluorescent green, we talked of the Washoe who lived in the Tahoe Basin, which led to my daughter telling me that from just before the Gold Rush until around 1873, the population of Native Americans in California declined from 150,000 to 30,000. She told me about the Act for the Government and Protection of Indians, signed into law in 1850 by the state's first governor, sanctioning the murder and enslavement of Native Americans in the "free" state of California. "I didn't learn any of *that* in fourth grade history," my daughter said. Neither did I. Though I remember learning about the missions. We built replicas using sugar cubes and popsicle sticks. My daughter and I spent most of the day on the ridge, she keying the species she didn't know, me asking questions mostly to hear her talk about something she loved. I learned that paintbrush is a hemiparasite and that the blooms aren't flowers, but bracts, or specialized leaves. I told her that another common name for *Castilleja* is prairie fire.

> Over the grassland,
> through forest and desert—
> look where their faith spread.

IV

On the drive home, we crossed Donner Pass and my daughter asked if
I knew about Luis and Salvador, the two Miwoks who were shot and
consumed by other members of the Donner Party. I knew about this,
but I had forgotten the men's names. We descended into the foothills
then passed Auburn, onto the last straight miles down 80 into the valley,
watching the car's thermometer climb into the triple digits. That was
three years ago, and though I've thought about the wildflowers each year,
I've missed the bloom, the best part anyway, which has come earlier than
usual. If my daughter can come to visit this year, I'll try again.

Early April and across the street my neighbor is landscaping his yard with
drought-tolerant plants. A warm day, and he's working shirtless, digging
a hole for an ornamental juniper. Typically, 90% of California's rain
falls between the first of October and April. According to the Drought
Monitor, much of the state is already abnormally dry or experiencing
moderate drought. No rain in the forecast as far as they can predict, and
this past February was the driest on record.

> Asleep in my chair,
> I remember the flowers.
> Please tell me their names.

Wend *(After Raymond Carver)*

A cobweb hangs from my lamp—
                intricate, tethering air.
I lean close and its thin strand
                is disturbed by my breathing.
Before long, before anyone notices,
                I'll be gone from this place.

As it happens,

the anniversary of my birth is also
the anniversary of my father's death.
For years afterward, I refused

to celebrate, forbade my girlfriend,
now my wife, the giving of gifts,
the dining out, the cards.

It seemed unfair that loss
should hold my joy in check, or tip
some cosmic scale toward dark.

But I had changed. I remember when
the news came I stood stone still,
my body sclerotic as his heart.

And when, at last, I could move again,
a hardness remained.
Call it the legacy of pain.

As it happens, my son is twenty-two,
the age I was when my old man died.
I've done my best to love him and

to teach him not to fear the end.
But he has witnessed my gradual slide—
the loss of strength, the shorter stride.

The truth is plain though I have tried
to conceal it; the weight and waste and
disappointment and regret are facts

that he already senses. I can feel it
when I embrace him—
the way his body tenses.

Inside the Circle

When, in the soft effulgence of fire, voices
               die down and the smoke that is change
     wafts starward through a canopy of shadow,

               each attendant leans into the bygone choices
     that have led him there—his own charred
manshape cast off into night. Then,

     all unity gone, each one gazes into self,
               hearkens to wood's molten word, his ears
fearful of hearing the hiss of his singed image.

Proselytus

The heron has no need of heaven,
not when ankling above its own blurred image bent
back by light upon the river's skin,
nor when the prayer of its patient waiting
hones hunger to an angel and
the river's liquid shiver ceases, nor when,
without anger, its chaste brain drives at once, beyond
the abducting eye, its yellow bill-spear
down, through its mirrored surface self into
that other world of blood and flesh.

Fish and frogs attend it, and ducklings
dabble within the shadow of its slaty cloak,
open to enfold their new-hatched and
immaculate death. The heron troubles the water
where I have come at dawn, entering late
to answer, with the others, its voiceless
summons stalking the fog. I walk the river's
willowed, reedy rim, where rime has left
the smooth rocks slick. There, as I slip
and pick my blunted way with care, I hear

the heron lift its vast-winged weight aloft
and know that I have strayed too near, and see
shrouded in a downed cloud's breath,
its apparition rise, take flight, unhurried
and sure, beyond the farther shore where
I cannot follow. There, it will descend, tall-
shouldered, crowned, to minster
to the mice and voles that mine the mead.
And I am left with my need, unable to read
the runed sand where a god stood.

Balm

The pear tree breaks out in bees.

        The wind goes nattering on.

I don't move. I let the wind speak.

        I listen and the wind asks,

"Isn't God the youngest pear tree?"

        Salvation is a simple thing.

Chant

The sounds as they appear to you are not only different from those that are really present, but they sometimes behave so strangely as to seem quite impossible.

—Diana Deutsch

Sounds sometimes behave so strangely
that we hear music when it isn't there.
Sounds sometimes behave so strangely

that we hear words in music, arranged
by the brain where no words were.
Sounds sometimes behave so strangely

that the nature of all things is mainly
present. The opened ear becomes the seer.
Sounds sometimes behave so strangely:

"Here is my beauty, here is my glee,"
the oriole said. That's what Emerson's wife heard.
Sounds sometimes behave so strangely

that the ambient world speaks to us, changing
landscape back to its topology of prayer.
Sounds sometimes behave so strangely

as to open a door. "Here's my beauty,
here's my glee," the oriole announces, sure
that his hearers will use their senses truly

so that ear and earth cohere. Strangely,
we are estranged from the mundane. Pure
sounds sometimes behave so. Strangely,

we forget this. O oriole, don't let me.
Speak the impossible so that I may hear
sounds sometimes behave so strangely,
sounds sometimes behave so strangely.

Unto This Day

After the thundersnow, when the cell-latch
lifted, I kissed the ones I loved and fled
into the crystal hills, where blue on white

and white on blue, my liquid eyes breathed
arias of ice. I left a shallow track, and when
new snow began to fall, I looked back

and saw each footprint was a prayer
that only memory's tracing could keep clear.
Love's frigid vigil held me there

until all rote relinquishments were healed.
Lost and full of promise, I could not move
to mar my hope in what I had not seen.

Thence when I woke to waking, I was home,
hopeful and devoured. And no one knew me there.

Written

a snail this morning
       ascending the pumpkin,
           does not need me

              to come into being
         this other
      element that shines

something out of sight
       my friend, (for our use
          only) all creation is

              vanishing script, what
                  was it or was it
                     writing it was

                     writing, I saw my own
              child's eye shine
           from the surface of Sugar Creek

              where water turned
                  over slickrock my first
                     invertebrate book

Scale

A table seems to grow small
                as we move away from it.
The object—table, tree, or house—
                outside the mind remains unchanged.
I saw God, in his wee immensity, looking
                through my late eyes, not with them.

The Cause

Climbing out of Hades,
        Orpheus thought of all he'd done,
                of how he'd sung his course
                        past Cerberus, left Sisyphus sitting
                                on his rock, stalled Ixion's fiery wheel,
                        eased the thirsty curse of Tantalus,
                sluiced the Furies' arid cheeks,
        turned the Belides from their dripping
                sieves, and saved Tityus' liver
                        from the buzzard beaks awhile.

                        He smiled remembering
                noble mouths unfrown
        as Pluto and his queen gazed
down from their dark thrones,
unable to refuse his plea. All this
        he'd done through desire
                born of loss. He saw that now.
                        The poet's true muse isn't love,
                                it's lack. It caused his fame.
                        It was his cause, an endless source
                of song. Nearly out,

                        he paused.

Allure

A hawk sits hidden,
          conspicuously and most high
     upon a lamp post,
red-shouldered
          as with blood bedight.

     In the day's exhausted
     light, its swivel-headed, arrow-
keen and earthward gaze
     surveys the evening
     gold grown over the rush
          hour crush of cars, where

locked in traffic, I break,
          creep forward, break,
     until—some nameless
progress fulfilled—I pass
at last, useless and low,
          beneath that huge disdain

and feel some puling
          part of me flushed forth
     from the sheltering
roadside ditchgrass, skeltering
          and blind, to be
          seized in the talons
     of that terrible sight.

     Inviolable good has drawn
my busted eyes into

the mirror of my passing,
where plume-sheen
dazzles in last-light,
and my ravening,
parched heart leaps

into the air.

Notes

The six-line poems in this book are English approximations of *sijo*, a traditional Korean form that originated during the Goryeo dynasty (918-1392) and is still being written today. Syllabic in structure, the three lines of a sijo are broken into two hemistiches. There is a shift at the beginning of the third line similar to the volta of a sonnet. For those interested in the form, I recommend *The Bamboo Grove: An Introduction to Sijo*, edited and translated by Richard Rutt.

Page 14, "Thaw": The line "Two trout lie gutted in new snow" is a slight modification of a line from Jack Driscoll's "After Ice Fishing on West Bay."

Page 18, "How I Lost My Voice" is for Peter Grandbois.

Page 21, "Lesson": This poem draws liberally from a passage in Yamamoto Tsunetomo's *Hagakure*, translated by William Scott Wilson.

Page 26, "Credential": "All this was a long time ago, / I remember," and "But set down this, set down this" are passages borrowed from T.S. Eliot's poem, "Journey of the Magi."

Page 34, "When Paradise Burned" is for Joanne Allred.

Page 44, "Homage to Thomas Traherne in the Pyrocene": In 1967, the manuscript of Thomas Traherne's *Commentaries of Heaven* was rescued from a burning rubbish heap in England by a man looking for car parts.

Page 54, "The Funeral of Shelley": For an account of P.B. Shelley's funeral, in all its grisly detail, see *Recollections of the Last Days of Shelley and Bryon* by Edward John Trelawny (1792-1881).

Page 76, "Proselytus": Late Latin proselytes, from Greek *prosēlytos* "convert (to Judaism), stranger," literally "one who has come over."

ACKNOWLEDGMENTS

The author would like to thank the editors of the journals in which these poems first appeared.

Bicoastal Review: "Dream #37"
Boulevard: "Anniversary"
Delmarva Review: "Wend (*After Raymond Carver*)," "Balm," and "Stone Sijo"
88: A Journal of Contemporary American Poetry: "(as)under"
Faultline: "When Paradise Burned"
Gold Man Review: "Shade"
Marsh Hawk Review: "As it happens"
Matador Review: "Novum"
The Missouri Review: "Proselytus"
Mixer: "A Prognosis"
The National Poetry Review: "Why I Sleep in My Best Suit"
Phantom Drift Limited: "Omen"
Plume Poetry Journal: "Scale"
Portland Review: "Fabric"
Red Rock Review Literary Journal: "The Word"
Reservoir Road Review: "How I Lost My Voice"
Rhino: "Nursery"
Roanoke Review: "Copula"
Route 7 Review: "Psalm"
Seneca Review: "Chant"
Split Rock Review: "Patriotism"
Stone Poetry Quarterly: "Catechism" and "The Cause"
The Stillwater Review: "Un-Selfie"
Strange Machine: "Null Choir"
Superstition [Review]: "Jubliate" and "Thaw"
Sweet: "March"

Thirteen Bridges Review: "American Idiom," "Credential," and "Unto This Day"

Tomahawk Creek Review: "Allure" and "Written"

Trace Fossils Review: "Waiting to View the Corpse Flower"

VOLT: "*In Perpetuum*" and "Suzerain"

The author also wishes to thank the following people for their continued friendship, guidance, and support: Matthew Cooperman, Tim Kahl, Susan Kelly-DeWitt, Forrest Gander, Peter Grandbois, Brenda Hillman, Bin Ramke, Donald Revell, Elizabeth Robinson, and Randy White. Special thanks to Jennifer Sweeney, who distinguished the river from its tributaries. And grateful acknowledgement to Samuli Heimonen for loaning me his *Angel*.

About the Poet

Joshua McKinney, winner of the first John Ridland Poetry Prize, is the author of four previous poetry collections: *Small Sillion* (Parlor Press, 2019), *Mad Cursive* (Wordcraft of Oregon, 2012), *The Novice Mourner*, winner of the Dorothy Brunsman Poetry Prize (Bear Star Press, 2005), and *Saunter*, winner of the Contemporary Poetry Series Competition (University of Georgia, 2002). Professor Emeritus of English at California State University, Sacramento, he co-edits the online ecopoetics journal, *Clade Song*.

Also from

Gunpowder Press

Frangible Operas, poems by Susan Kelly-DeWitt
Before Traveling to Alabama, poems by David Case
Mother Lode, poems by Peg Quinn
Raft of Days, poems by Catherine Abbey Hodges
Unfinished City, poems by Nan Cohen
Original Face, poems by Jim Peterson
Shaping Water, poems by Barry Spacks
The Tarnation of Faust, poems by David Case
Mouth & Fruit, poems by Chryss Yost

CALIFORNIA POETS SERIES

Downtime, poems by Gary Soto
Speech Crush, poems by Sandra McPherson
Our Music, poems by Dennis Schmitz
Gatherer's Alphabet, poems by Susan Kelly-DeWitt

DRYDEN-VREELAND BOOK PRIZE

Three-Day Weekend, poems by Christopher Blackman

Printed in the USA
CPSIA information can be obtained
at www.ICGtesting.com
LVHW090049200724
785535LV00006B/20